Dedicated to my son, Kale.

My name is Kale and
I always think for myself.

Especially around bullies.

When my friend Sarah came to school
last week with her shirt on backwards
Mikey and his friends laughed at her.

I'm Kale and I know that's bullying, so I told
her I did the same thing the week before.
That made her smile and we laughed about it
while we walked away to the craft table.

When my classmate Cara walked back from the bathroom, she had a long piece of toilet paper dragging from her shoe. Mikey whispered in my ear that we shouldn't tell her and see how long it takes for her to notice.

I'm Kale and I know that's bullying, so I told Mikey that he probably wouldn't like that if it were him. Then I quickly went and pulled it off Cara's shoe for her. She didn't even notice.

When Sarah first got her glasses,
Mikey called her four-eyes.

I'm Kale and I know that's bullying. I told her that
I wished I could wear glasses! I would pick out
bright green ones to match my green dinosaur
shoes. Then I told her that the purple ones
she picked out looked really good on her.

When Cara came to school after Christmas showing off her new big pink hair bow, Mikey told her that only babies wear bows in their hair.

I'm Kale and I know that's bullying, so I told her that's not true. My older sister wears a bow in her hair all the time and she's super cool.

During recess Mikey and his friends were all throwing snowballs at Jason, even though he was asking them to stop.

I'm Kale and I know that's bullying, so I quickly let the teacher know and she put a stop to it. Then I asked Jason if he'd like to help me build my snow fort.

In class I overheard all the girls telling Sarah that she couldn't be in their club because she didn't have a unicorn shirt like the rest of them.

I'm Kale and I know that's bullying, so I told Sarah that she doesn't want to be in a club like that anyways. Then I suggested we try to do the new puzzle that Mrs. Grey brought in that day.

On the bus Mikey laughed at Jason because he was sitting all alone. He was getting other kids to laugh and call him names too.

I'm Kale and I know that's bullying, so I got up from my seat and went to sit with Jason. I showed him my new find-and-seek dinosaur book and told him that we should just ignore Mikey.

On the playground Cara and Jason were on the tire swing and Cara was saying that she wanted to get off. Mikey kept pushing the tire higher and higher until Cara started to cry.

I'm Kale and I know that's bullying so I ran over to tell Mikey to stop and I slowed down the swing as quickly as I could so Cara could get off. Mikey told me I was ruining his fun, but I just told him that he was the only one having fun.

During craft time Mikey took all the markers from the middle and said they were all for him. Sara was left without any markers and I needed the green one for the tree I was coloring.

I'm Kale and I know that's bullying, so I told Mikey he had to put all the markers back and just take the one he was using. He didn't like that very much, so I had to ask Mrs. Gray for some help. She got Mikey to go read a book with her since he couldn't seem to share.

At recess we played pirate ship and Mikey was being bossy trying to tell everyone what part to play. He told me I would play the part of the Captain's pet dog, but I didn't want to do that.

I'm Kale and I know that's bullying, so I stood up tall and said I was going to pick my own character to play and so should everybody else. Mikey sighed but he knew I wasn't giving in, so he agreed.

My name is Kale and I always stand up for myself and my friends around bullies. If that doesn't work, then I walk away or ask an adult for help. It's great to always think for myself.

Hello Readers!

I hope your little ones learned some
great tips from this book!

I would love to know what you thought. I am an Indie
Author and Amazon reviews are a **HUGE DEAL** to me!

If you have a moment to leave this book a quick
review, **YOU WOULD MAKE MY DAY!**

Thank you so much!

Kristy Hammill